The Official Celtic
Football Club Annual 2011
Written by Joe Sullivan & Mark Henderson

A Grange Publication

© 2010. Published by Grange Communications Ltd., Edinburgh, under licence from Celtic Football Club. Printed in the EU.

Photographs © Angus Johnston, Alan Whyte,
Press Association Images, Thinkstock & SNS Group

ISBN 978-1-907104-60-2

£7.99

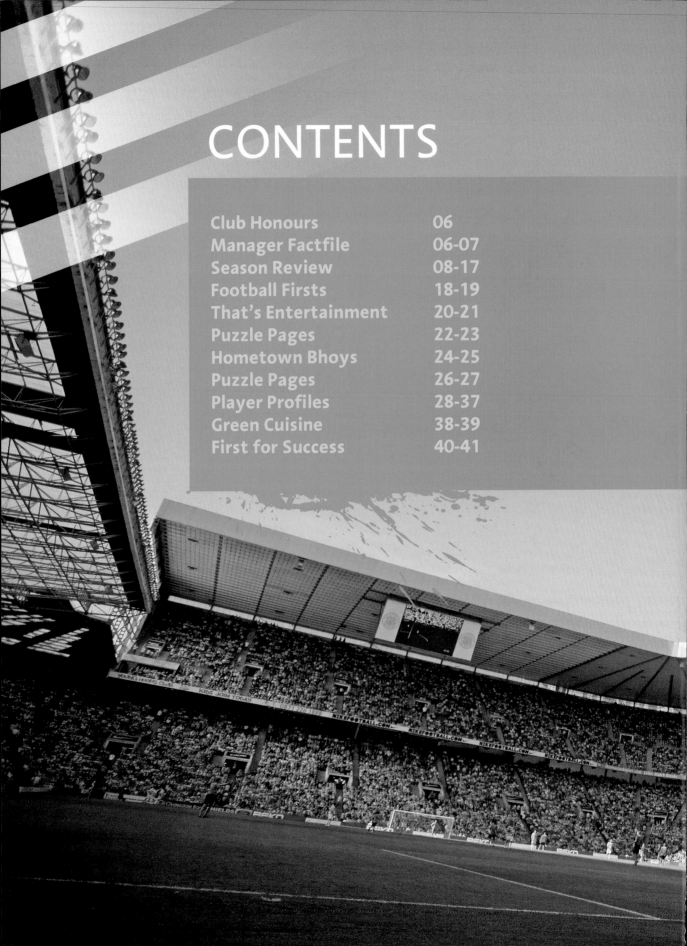

CONTENTS

CLUB HONOURS

Scottish League Winners [42 times]

1892/93, 1893/94, 1895/96, 1897/98, 1904/05, 1905/06, 1906/07, 1907/08, 1908/09, 1909/10, 1913/14, 1914/15, 1915/16, 1916/17, 1918/19, 1921/22, 1925/26, 1935/36, 1937/38, 1953/54, 1965/66, 1966/67, 1967/68, 1968/69, 1969/70, 1970/71, 1971/72, 1972/73, 1973/74, 1976/77, 1978/79, 1980/81, 1981/82, 1985/86, 1987/88, 1997/98, 2000/01, 2001/02, 2003/04, 2005/06, 2006/07, 2007/08

Scottish Cup Winners [34 times]

1892, 1899, 1900, 1904, 1907, 1908, 1911, 1912, 1914, 1923, 1925, 1927, 1931, 1933, 1937, 1951, 1954, 1965, 1967, 1969, 1971, 1972, 1974, 1975, 1977, 1980, 1985, 1988, 1989, 1995, 2001, 2004, 2005, 2007

League Cup Winners [14 times]

1956/57, 1957/58, 1965/66, 1966/67, 1967/68, 1968/69, 1969/70, 1974/75, 1982/83, 1997/98, 1999/00, 2000/01, 2005/06, 2008/09

European Cup Winners 1967

Coronation Cup Winners 1953

MANAGER FACTFILE
Neil Lennon

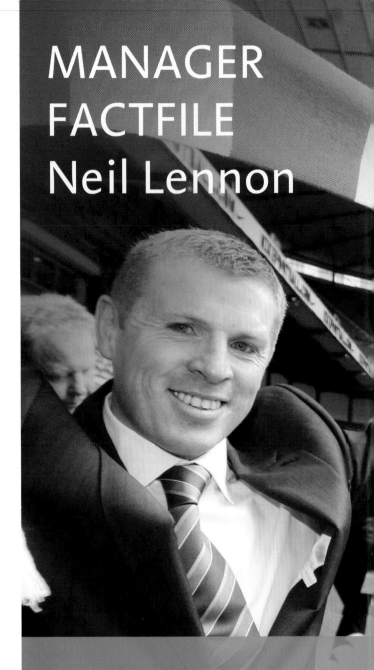

NEIL LENNON achieved his dream on the pitch as a Celtic player. Like many youngsters from the Emerald Isle, he always wanted to play for the club, but, significantly, wanted to be remembered as a winner. A quick scan of the impressive array of medals he collected with the Hoops proves that his wishes were fulfilled. Over seven seasons, the Irishman won five league championships, three Scottish Cups and two League Cups. There are few who can boast of such feats.

Lennon has transferred that winning mentality into his coaching – firstly, as a first-team coach under Gordon Strachan, and then while in charge of Celtic's Development Squad. When Tony Mowbray departed as manager last March, Lennon was asked to take the reins until the end of the season. He responded by galvanising the squad and securing eight successive league wins on the spin.

So when the club began the process of appointing a permanent replacement early in the summer,

D.O.B: 25/06/71

Born: Lurgan

Playing career record:
Manchester City (1989-90),
Crewe Alexandra (1990-96),
Leicester City (1996-2000),
Celtic (2000-07),
Nottingham Forest (2007-08),
Wycombe Wanderers (2008).

Playing honours:
Leicester City - League Cup Winners:
(1996/97, 1999/00)

Celtic - Scottish Premier League Champions:
(2000/01, 2001/02, 2003/04, 2005/06, 2006/07)

Scottish Cup Winners:
(2001, 2004, 2007)

Scottish League Cup Winners:
(2000/01, 2005/06)

UEFA Cup Runners-up:
(2002/03)

Lennon's credentials fitted the bill perfectly for taking the club forward and back to the top of Scottish football. On June 9, 2010, he was confirmed as the new manager of Celtic.

He may be young in the managerial age stakes, but Lennon has learned his trade during a long and illustrious playing career under some of the finest managers in British football.

After leaving Manchester City as a teenager, he signed for Dario Gradi's Crewe Alexandra, spending six seasons there, before being snapped up by Martin O'Neill at Leicester City.

Lennon enjoyed a remarkable spell of success under his countryman at Filbert Street. After winning promotion to the Premier League, the Foxes established themselves in England's top flight with a series of top 10 finishes and lifted two League Cups.

When O'Neill moved north to take charge of Celtic in 2000, Lennon quickly followed him, becoming a pivotal part of the Celtic side which went on to dominate Scottish football over the ensuing years. Single-minded and fiercely competitive, Lennon made 304 appearances in the Hoops, many of those as club captain, and won every domestic honour. He also starred in the side that enjoyed the memorable run to the UEFA Cup final in 2003.

In 2005, O'Neill left, but his successor, Gordon Strachan, was another admirer of Lennon's abilities. Over the next two years, Lennon secured further silverware until his departure from the club in 2007. His absence wouldn't be for long, though, and he was soon back at Celtic Park – this time an animated presence on the touchline.

Now in charge of the Hoops, Lennon will be aiming to replicate the success he enjoyed as a player and see Celtic Football Club back on the trophy trail.

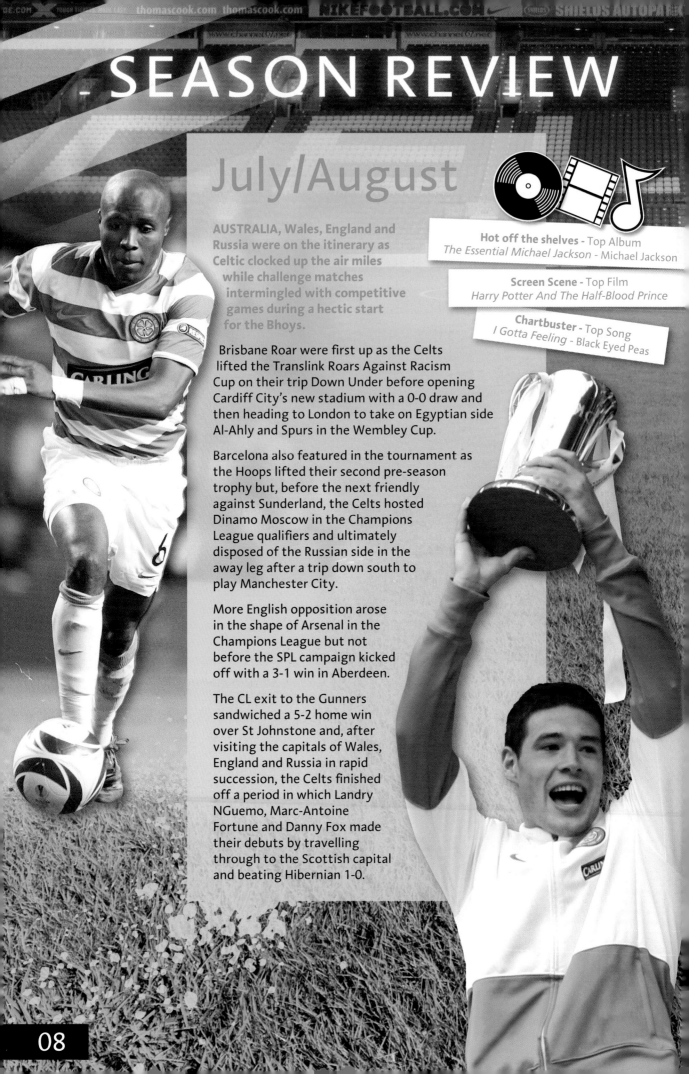

SEASON REVIEW

July/August

AUSTRALIA, Wales, England and Russia were on the itinerary as Celtic clocked up the air miles while challenge matches intermingled with competitive games during a hectic start for the Bhoys.

Brisbane Roar were first up as the Celts lifted the Translink Roars Against Racism Cup on their trip Down Under before opening Cardiff City's new stadium with a 0-0 draw and then heading to London to take on Egyptian side Al-Ahly and Spurs in the Wembley Cup.

Barcelona also featured in the tournament as the Hoops lifted their second pre-season trophy but, before the next friendly against Sunderland, the Celts hosted Dinamo Moscow in the Champions League qualifiers and ultimately disposed of the Russian side in the away leg after a trip down south to play Manchester City.

More English opposition arose in the shape of Arsenal in the Champions League but not before the SPL campaign kicked off with a 3-1 win in Aberdeen.

The CL exit to the Gunners sandwiched a 5-2 home win over St Johnstone and, after visiting the capitals of Wales, England and Russia in rapid succession, the Celts finished off a period in which Landry NGuemo, Marc-Antoine Fortune and Danny Fox made their debuts by travelling through to the Scottish capital and beating Hibernian 1-0.

Hot off the shelves - Top Album
The Essential Michael Jackson - Michael Jackson

Screen Scene - Top Film
Harry Potter And The Half-Blood Prince

Chartbuster - Top Song
I Gotta Feeling - Black Eyed Peas

September

THE month kicked-off with a young team travelling to Canada to take on Portuguese side Benfica and the Celts squeezed in a 1-1 home draw with Dundee United before jetting off to Israel to take on Hapoel Tel-Aviv in the Europa League.

Lukasz Zaluska and Niall McGinn were the September debutants and the Hoops returned from a bruising 2-1 defeat in Israel and showed tremendous character to take all three points with a 2-1 victory over Hearts, thanks to Glenn Loovens' dramatic injury-time winner.

The Hoops continued that good form into the two remaining fixtures in September.

Falkirk were dispatched comfortably in the League Cup in a 4-0 rout, which was marked by Paddy McCourt's first goal for the club. And what a goal it was.

Collecting a pass in his own half, he waltzed past the entire Bairns defence before coolly chipping the ball over Robert Olejnik and into the net.

The 'Derry Pele' show continued at the weekend in the SPL match with St Mirren. Celtic emerged with the spoils after a hard-fought win in Paisley, but it was McCourt who again lit-up proceedings. In a clone of his strike just days earlier, he picked up the ball on the half-way line and skipped past several challenges, before finishing into the far corner.

Hot off the shelves - Top Album
Humbug - Arctic Monkeys

Screen Scene - Top Film
Cloudy With A Chance Of Meatballs

Chartbuster - Top Song
Holiday - Dizzee Rascal

October

CELTIC began the month back on Europa League duty as they hosted old foes Rapid Vienna for the first time since the controversial European Cup-Winners' Cup meeting in 1984.

After a feverish build-up, the match ended 1-1 with Scott McDonald cancelling out the Austrian side's early opener to give the Hoops their first point in the group.

Just three days later, the Hoops travelled to Ibrox to contest their first Glasgow derby of the season and were unfortunate to get no reward for their efforts in a 2-1 defeat.

The Celts looked to get back on track with the visit of Motherwell but were left frustrated after a 0-0 draw only netted a point.

It was a similar story in the next Europa League outing against Hamburg. Despite creating several openings, a Marcus Berg strike gave the German side a 1-0 victory.

Hot off the shelves - Top Album
Brand New Eyes - Paramore

Screen Scene - Top Film
Up

Chartbuster - Top Song
Oopsy Daisy - Chipmunk

At the weekend, Celtic were back on league duty and secured a much-needed three points when goals from Shaun Maloney and McDonald sealed a 2-1 win over Hamilton.

Any hopes of retaining the League Cup were extinguished though, after a narrow defeat to Hearts.

But the month ended on a more positive note as goals from Aiden McGeady, Georgios Samaras and Niall McGinn saw Kilmarnock swept aside in a 3-0 victory.

10

November

AFTER the hectic run of games in the previous month, Celtic's schedule eased off in November when only four fixtures took place.

First up was a trip to Hamburg for a tough Europa League clash. The Hoops created several good goal-scoring chances but had to settle for a credible 0-0 draw.

It was then back to SPL duty as Celtic visited struggling Falkirk, who shocked Celtic by producing their best performance of the season and taking a share of the spoils in a six-goal thriller.

Up next was a difficult trip to Tannadice to take on Dundee United. An improved performance was rewarded when Barry Robson gave Celtic the lead from the penalty spot, but the home side struck twice in the final 10 minutes to take maximum points and leave the Hoops stunned.

A win was vital in Celtic's only home fixture of the month against St Mirren and it was duly delivered through a double from Scott McDonald and a Georgios Samaras strike in a 3-1 triumph.

Hot off the shelves - Top Album
Echo - Leona Lewis

Screen Scene - Top Film
A Christmas Carol

Chartbuster - Top Song
Meet Me Halfway - Black Eyed Peas

11

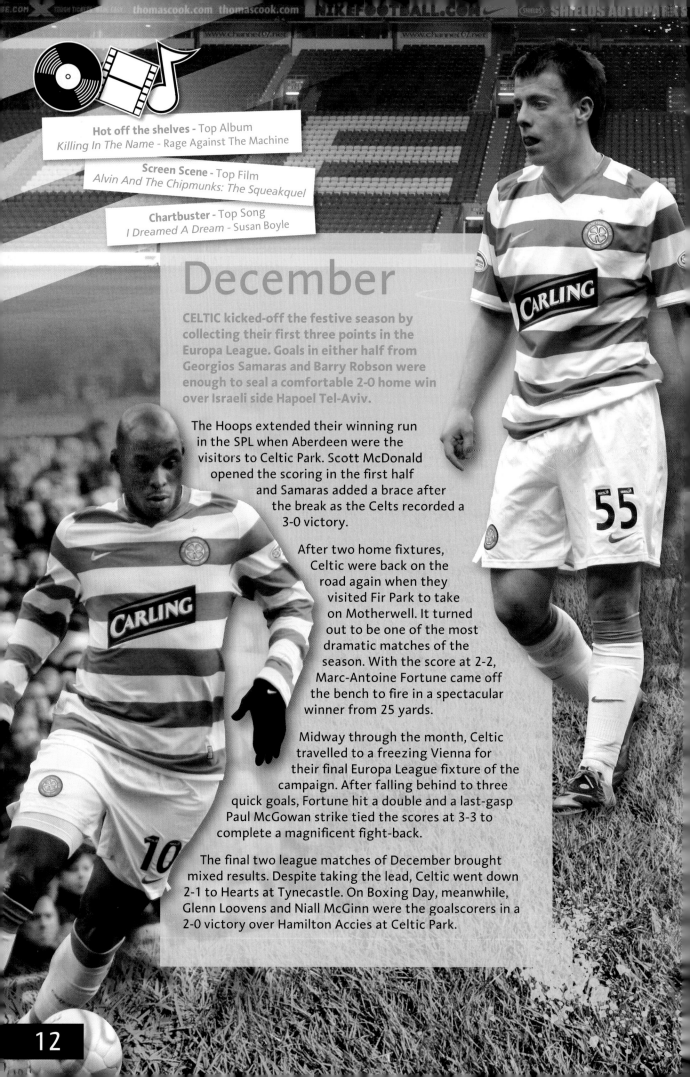

December

CELTIC kicked-off the festive season by collecting their first three points in the Europa League. Goals in either half from Georgios Samaras and Barry Robson were enough to seal a comfortable 2-0 home win over Israeli side Hapoel Tel-Aviv.

The Hoops extended their winning run in the SPL when Aberdeen were the visitors to Celtic Park. Scott McDonald opened the scoring in the first half and Samaras added a brace after the break as the Celts recorded a 3-0 victory.

After two home fixtures, Celtic were back on the road again when they visited Fir Park to take on Motherwell. It turned out to be one of the most dramatic matches of the season. With the score at 2-2, Marc-Antoine Fortune came off the bench to fire in a spectacular winner from 25 yards.

Midway through the month, Celtic travelled to a freezing Vienna for their final Europa League fixture of the campaign. After falling behind to three quick goals, Fortune hit a double and a last-gasp Paul McGowan strike tied the scores at 3-3 to complete a magnificent fight-back.

The final two league matches of December brought mixed results. Despite taking the lead, Celtic went down 2-1 to Hearts at Tynecastle. On Boxing Day, meanwhile, Glenn Loovens and Niall McGinn were the goalscorers in a 2-0 victory over Hamilton Accies at Celtic Park.

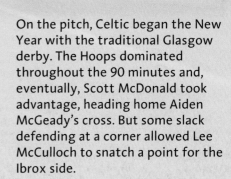

January

THE catchword around Celtic Park in January was change. The opening of the transfer window was the catalyst for several arrivals and departures among the Hoops squad.

The highest-profile signing was, of course, Irish star Robbie Keane, who dramatically moved from Spurs on loan right on the cusp of February. He followed Diomansy Kamara, Edson Braafheid, Morten Rasmussen, Jos Hooiveld, Thomas Rogne, Ki Sung-Yueng and youngster Paul Slane onto the Celtic books.

Out the exit door, meanwhile, went Gary Caldwell, Steven McManus, Scott McDonald, Danny Fox, Willo Flood, Mark Brown and Chris Killen.

On the pitch, Celtic began the New Year with the traditional Glasgow derby. The Hoops dominated throughout the 90 minutes and, eventually, Scott McDonald took advantage, heading home Aiden McGeady's cross. But some slack defending at a corner allowed Lee McCulloch to snatch a point for the Ibrox side.

The next home match brought further disappointment as Falkirk held the Hoops to a 1-1 draw. In the Scottish Cup, though, Celtic progressed to the fourth round after Niall McGinn's goal gave them a 1-0 win over Morton.

With the cold snap decimating the SPL fixture list, the Celts faced three games in the space of a week at the end of the month. A double from Marc-Antoine Fortune and strikes from Georgios Samaras and Paddy McCourt sealed a 4-1 win over St Johnstone.

Another win looked likely when Fortune headed Celtic in front against Hibernian, but the Edinburgh side levelled proceedings and hit an injury-time winner to take all three points back along the M8. In the month's final match however, Rasmussen's first goal for the club did clinch a 1-0 win over Hamilton.

Hot off the shelves - Top Album
Lungs - Florence & The Machine

Screen Scene - Top Film
Avatar

Chartbuster - Top Song
Replay - Iyaz

February

JUST one day after the closure of the transfer window, Celtic took on Kilmarnock at Rugby Park, with many of the new Bhoys featuring within the starting XI.

However, the new-look Hoops were left to rue a number of missed chances as the Ayrshire side grabbed all three points in a 1-0 win.

On a brighter note, Celtic booked their place in the Scottish Cup quarter-final with a win over First Division

Hot off the shelves - Top Album
Sunny Side Up - Paolo Nutini

Screen Scene - Top Film
Valentine's Day

Chartbuster - Top Song
Everybody Hurts - Hope For Haiti

Dunfermline, with Robbie Keane and Diomansy Kamara netting their first goals for the club.

Back at Celtic Park, second-half strikes from Glenn Loovens and Marc-Antoine Fortune secured three points against Hearts. And, after Fortune, Kamara, Keane and Aiden McGeady built a 4-2 lead up at Aberdeen, it seemed Celtic were about to chalk up another league win, but two late goals for the Dons saw them steal a point.

A Keane goal was enough to sink Dundee United at Celtic Park, before the Glasgow derby at Ibrox. The match was goal-less when Scott Brown was controversially ordered off and the Hoops were cruelly denied a point when Maurice Edu stabbed home a late winner.

March

THIS proved to be somewhat of a turbulent month at Celtic with Tony Mowbray's eight-month reign as manager coming to an abrupt end.

Initially, Robbie Keane provided some tonic to the derby defeat to Rangers with both goals in an away win at Falkirk.

The Irishman went one better the following week at Rugby Park, hitting a wonderful hat-trick, as the Hoops progressed to the Scottish Cup semi-final with a 3-0 win over Kilmarnock.

There was a repeat of that scoreline when St Johnstone visited Celtic Park as Keane, Josh Thompson and Georgios Samaras found the net without reply.

With three wins and three clean sheets on the trot, the 4-0 reversal to St Mirren left everyone stunned and, the next day, Mowbray departed the club, along with backroom staff, Mark Venus and Peter Grant.

Neil Lennon, who had been coaching the development squad, took over as interim manager for the rest of the season. Former Celtic team-mate Johan Mjallby flew in from Sweden to assist him.

The new team got off to a winning start against Kilmarnock, guiding the Hoops to a 3-1 triumph thanks to two goals from Keane and another from Scott Brown.

Hot off the shelves - Top Album
Brother - Boyzone

Screen Scene - Top Film
Alice In Wonderland

Chartbuster - Top Song
Pass Out - Tinie Tempah

15

April

CELTIC enjoyed their best winning run in the SPL during April, but the month would, unfortunately, be dominated by one result.

On Easter Sunday, the Hoops travelled through to the capital and came out on top in a hard-fought encounter with Hibernian. A second-half penalty from Robbie Keane proved to be the difference between the sides.

However, the next result in the Scottish Cup semi-final effectively dashed any expectations Celtic still had for picking up silverware that season. In a forgettable day at Hampden, the Hoops exited the competition after a 2-0 defeat to First Division Ross County.

But Lennon's side recovered well from that setback and showed good character to win their next three league games. Josh Thompson struck twice to see off Motherwell, before Morten Rasmussen stabbed home a late winner in a dramatic 3-2 victory over Hibernian.

Celtic saved their best performance of the month for a crucial clash with Dundee United at Tannadice. Goals in either half from Diomansy Kamara and Keane deservedly saw off the Terrors and, significantly, secured second spot in the SPL.

Hot off the shelves - Top Album
The Fame - Lady Gaga

Screen Scene - Top Film
Clash Of The Titans

Chartbuster - Top Song
This Ain't A Love Song - Scouting For Girls

May

BRIMMING with confidence from five SPL victories on the spin, Celtic continued their impressive form in May to finish the season on a high note.

The opening match of the month saw Motherwell emphatically put to the sword at Celtic Park in a 4-0 rout. Aiden McGeady opened the scoring with a sublime chip, before Darren O'Dea nodded in the second. There was a memorable debut for James Forrest, who came off the bench to score with a well-executed shot. Keane added his obligatory goal in added time to round off an excellent team performance.

In the final Glasgow derby of the season, the Hoops restored some much-needed pride by beating Rangers 2-1 at Celtic Park. After a heavy spell of pressure, Lee Naylor fired home a free-kick to open the scoring. Kenny Miller equalised for the Ibrox side, but Marc-Antoine Fortune nodded home the winner just before half-time.

There would be a tough encounter with Hearts at Tynecastle to finish the season, but the Hoops were determined to rack up their eighth SPL win in a row.

Keane showed good composure to put the Hoops in front, grabbing his 16th goal for the club in the process. Although Hearts drew level, Chinese midfielder Zheng Zhi struck a stunning second-half winner to ensure the Celts signed off the campaign with another three points.

Hot off the shelves - Top Album
The Defamation Of Strickland Banks - Plan B

Screen Scene - Top Film
Iron Man 2

Chartbuster - Top Song
Good Times - Roll Deep

Football Firsts

YOU'VE seen your Celtic heroes take to the hallowed turf, resplendent in the Hoops and wearing the best football boots available – but what did they start out with?

Now is your chance to find out as we sat down with some of your favourite players to quiz them on some of their football firsts...

And some of them may not be very different from yours so see if any of their answers match up with yours.

Darren O'Dea

What was the first football match you attended?

It would be an Irish match against Liechtenstein at Lansdowne Road. I don't remember the score. I think it was maybe 1-0 to Ireland. I remember it was a poor game.

What was the first football strip you ever wore?

I think my first strip was an Ireland strip. It would have been in 1992 or thereabouts when I was about five-years-old.

Do you remember the first pair of football boots you had?

The first ones I ever had were a pair of Hi-Tecs. I was very young. It was probably when I first started playing football. But the ones I can really remember the most were a pair of red Asics boots.

Who was the first player you really admired?

Ryan Giggs. I loved watching him play. I supported Manchester United and Celtic as a boy, but Ryan Giggs was always the player I admired.

What was the first team you ever played for?

The first team I played for were Granada FC. They were a very local team to me. I started when I was six and then left at 11 and went to Home Farm.

Paddy McCourt

What was the first football match you attended?

The first game that I went to was Derry City v Dundalk and I think the score was 2-0. I was about 10.

What was the first football strip you ever wore?

My first top was a Celtic one. I can't remember exactly when, but it would have been about the mid-'90s.

Do you remember the first pair of football boots you had?

The first pair of football boots I had was a pair of Hi-Tecs. I must have been about four when I got them.

Who was the first player you really admired?

The first player I really admired was my older brother Harry. He played for Derry City as well.

What was the first team you ever played for?

Foyle Harps. I started with them when I was about eight and stayed with them for another eight years until I was 16.

Josh Thompson

What was the first football match you attended?

I think it was watching Stockport actually. When I first signed for them as a kid I got free tickets and got to go. I had never been to a match before, although I can't remember who they were playing that day.

What was the first football strip you ever wore?

My first strip was a Liverpool one. I think it was the away one. I can't remember exactly what one it was. But I would have it when I was about four, so around 1995.

Do you remember the first pair of football boots you had?

My first pair would have been when I was five or six and I got a pair of big massive Umbros

Who was the first player you really admired?

Michael Owen. I have a signed photograph from him. I got it for Christmas when I was younger and then I loved him from then on.

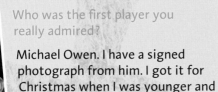

What was the first team you ever played for?

It was a team called Bury Rangers. I joined them when I was about seven or so. I only stayed there a year, because I started with Stockport when I was about eight.

Mark Wilson

What was the first football match you attended?

The first one I can ever remember is Celtic beating Rangers 2-1. You are going back to the early '90s and I remember John Collins scored. I went to the game with my dad. It was brilliant.

What was the first football strip you ever wore?

The first one would have been Celtic. I had all the tops even from the '80s. But my favourite was the Bumble Bee one. I remember getting it on my birthday.

Do you remember the first pair of football boots you had?

The first decent pair I had were the Ryan Giggs Reebok ones which were going about at time. They were black with the red marks on them. I loved them.

Who was the first player you really admired?

I would say Giggs, He was the star player at the time and I used to love watching him when I was younger.

What was the first team you ever played for?

The first team I played for were Burntbroom, who were a local boys' club team and I went on to play for Wolves Boys' Club after that.

To catch up on some more of your Celtic Football Firsts, turn to pages 48/49.

That's Entertainment

YOU may get some of your enjoyment boost from watching the Hoops playing but what about the men who are entertaining you – how do they get their kicks?

The big screen, the small screen, the stage and the iPod replace the football pitch as we ask the Celts want makes them Tic.

Lukasz Zaluska

What's your favourite piece of music on your iPod?

It just depends on my mood because sometimes I love to chill out. But sometimes when I am driving it's Limp Bizkit or heavy music.

Who is your favourite group/artist of all time?

I think Michael Jackson. His songs are great and everyone knows his music.

What was the best gig you have ever been to?

To be honest, I have only been twice to gigs, but last summer I went to see an old Polish rock 'n' roll group called Perfect back home. It was very nice and there were a lot of people there.

What is your favourite film?

I really like *Gladiator* and *Braveheart*. The last time I watched *Braveheart* with all my family without the subtitles and just the original version with all the Scottish accents and I really enjoyed it. I also like *300*.

What TV programme do you never miss?

I like *The Sopranos* and sometimes I like to watch the Polish League on Saturday evening. They show the highlights of the games and I like to watch my old teams from Poland.

Glenn Loovens

What's your favourite piece of music on your iPod?

I like Sade and Musiq Soulchild, which is a bit of R 'n' B. I listen a lot to those two.

Who is your favourite group/artist of all time?

Michael Jackson. He was pretty awesome. I am going to say him. I used to listen to him more than I do now, though.

What was the best gig you have ever been to?

The first concert I went to see was Michael Jackson in De Kuip, Rotterdam. I went with my family and was about seven. It was also the first time he took off on stage.

What is your favourite film?

I will say *Braveheart*. I always like movies played in ancient times about knights and Roman soldiers. But I also liked *Braveheart* because of the story.

What TV programme do you never miss?

I don't watch much TV to be honest, it's mostly films. On Sunday night, I watch the highlights of the football, but outside of that I wouldn't stay at home for anything in particular.

James Forrest

What's your favourite piece of music on your iPod?

Some stuff by U2

Who is your favourite group/artist of all time?

U2 again.

What was the best gig you have ever been to?

T in the Park. I also went to see Akon – he was pretty good.

What is your favourite film?

Law Abiding Citizen was one of the films I saw last season and it was really good.

What TV programme do you never miss?

Friends, I have always watched it growing up.

For more or your favourites' favourite stuff then turn to pages 42/43.

Spot the Difference

There are 12 differences between these pictures of Marc-Antoine Fortune heading in the winner against Rangers.

The first one has been circled, but can you spot the rest?

Answers on page 62

Season 2009/10 Quiz

01   What was the score in the first Celtic game Robbie Keane was involved in last season?

02   Lukasz Zaluska made his Celtic debut against which club?

03   Which Celt hit a double in the Hoops' first SPL game of the season?

04   What was Celtic's highest score of the season?

05   Celtic took part in only two 0-0 draws during the season. Who provided the opposition in the games?

06   Which 10 players scored their first goal for the club during the season?

07   Robbie Keane scored a hat-trick against which club?

08   How many players did Celtic use over the course of the season?

09   Which teams did Celtic play in London during the term?

10   How many capitals did Celtic play in?

How did you do? Find out with the answers on page 62.

OH GEE - IT'S IN THE BACK OF THE NET!

(Some Celtic own-goal gaffes)

One of the strangest Celtic own goals came in the long-lost Drybrough Cup back in 1974 when the Hoops were playing away at Airdrie. Keeper Denis Connaghan was about to throw the ball to Danny McGrain when he noticed the defender was being covered.

He changed his mind and tried to change direction in mid-throw and the ball ended up in the back of his own net.

Celtic still won 4-3, but talk about chucking one in!

23

Hometown Bhoys

GONE are the days when Celtic players were born and bred locally and even an east coast accent was considered exotic!

Nowadays, Hoops players come from all over the world and even some of the youth squad hail from far-flung countries.

So, we thought we'd ask them about their lives back home and find out what they miss the most about their hometown.

Andy Hinkel

What village/town/city are you from?

Leutenbach. It's a village about 20km north east of Stuttgart.

What do you miss most about it?

The food sometimes and some of the traditions they have in Germany, but I am very happy here.

Are you recognised when you go back there?

Yeah, I am always recognised when I go back home in that area around Stuttgart. If I go out for dinner or a drink, I have no privacy. But it's okay. I am from the area and I think people are proud that I went through the Stuttgart Academy and ended up playing for the national team.

What did you think about Scotland before you came here and what do you think now?

I had been a few times before I came here and it was always raining and grey, but now I know that sometimes there is sun as well – not that often though! But I think it is a great country. Scotland is a small country, but it's very famous throughout the world and I enjoy it here. Before I came I thought Glasgow would be an industrial city, but I really like it and you can have a nice life here.

Who is your local team and did you support them?

The biggest local team was Stuttgart and I supported them. So it was a dream come true when I played for them.

Dominic Cervi

What village/town/city are you from?

Norman, Oklahoma. In terms of population, there are about 120,000 people there.

What do you miss most about it?

The things I miss most about it are my friends and family.

Are you recognised when you go back there?

No, I don't get recognised. I will find out when I go back this year, but I don't think people will be stopping me in the street

What did you think about Scotland before you came here and what do you think now?

Before I came, when I thought of Scotland, it was kilts and Mel Gibson. Now I think of kilts and Mel Gibson, and lots of wet weather!

Who is your local team and did you support them?

We didn't really have a football team. The way it works back home is kind of like a youth system, but we were called the Norman Celtic. It was just like a development squad leading up to college. So I played for them.

Jos Hooiveld

What village/town/city are you from?

Groningen. It's in the north of Holland, it's not very big.

What do you miss most about it?

Family and friends because it's where I grew up.

Are you recognised when you go back there?

No, which is good.

What did you think about Scotland before you came here and what do you think now?

I expected it to be the way it is with nice-natured, good people. It's all lived up to expectations. I like the rough nature, all the hills and rivers.

Who is your local team and did you support them?

FC Groningen. I didn't really support them. When I was younger I backed them a little bit but I don't really support a team now. I prefer playing football to watching it.

Marc-Antoine Fortune

What village/town/city are you from?

Cayenne, which is the capital city of French Guiana.

What do you miss most about it?

I miss the way of life. It's more relaxed and everyone knows everyone. And, of course, I miss my family and friends.

Are you recognised when you go back there?

Yeah, not because I play football, though. It's just because I lived there and they know me. I have worked with a lot of the people there and played with them at school.

What did you think about Scotland before you came here and what do you think now?

I just knew about the weather. But, I think Glasgow and Edinburgh are nice cities. I have only been to those two, so those are the only ones I can talk about.

Who is your local team and did you support them?

I played for USL Montjoly and Club Colonial, so I supported them because I played for them.

For more inside info on the home joys of the Bhoys then turn to pages 58/59.

Maze

Celtic's Ki Sung-Yueng had to return to South Korea to pick up his kit before travelling to South Africa for the World Cup during the summer.

Can you help him get from Glasgow to Seoul and then on to Johannesburg?

START

FINISH

Answer on page 63

Celtic Quiz

QUIZ QUESTIONS

01 When Celtic won the European Cup in 1967, what connected the club's captain, manager and chairman?

02 Which top Portuguese team also wears the Hoops?

03 Which two trophies did Wim Jansen win in his season as manager?

04 Who has made the most appearances for Celtic ever?

05 Which Celt scored on his debut last season?

A	D	E	N	A	E	K	E	I	B	B	O	R
G	J	L	Q	E	T	U	O	P	Z	C	S	B
M	Z	W	R	Y	I	P	E	S	F	E	O	H
E	H	X	V	N	Q	N	E	T	T	E	U	U
L	E	O	A	D	A	D	G	A	J	B	T	L
T	N	Q	R	L	U	P	T	S	G	E	H	K
S	G	E	T	X	B	S	Q	E	Y	L	A	O
I	Z	Y	V	S	D	G	K	Z	V	B	F	M
H	H	N	C	E	S	E	F	Y	J	M	R	N
W	I	P	T	O	L	K	N	H	Y	U	I	G
S	R	I	F	Y	H	E	K	Q	P	B	C	X
X	N	U	H	A	L	Z	J	I	T	V	A	R
U	C	Z	A	X	U	T	H	T	H	R	E	E

WORDSEARCH

01 Arrived on loan from down south last season.

02 Where all the World Cup action was last summer

03 The number of Celts on the field.

04 The Hoops get a buzz in this strip.

05 The homeland of Dominic Cervi.

06 Scored Celtic's final goal of last season.

07 Spot-kick.

08 Magic number for hat-trick.

09 Blown at full-time.

Answers on pages 62/63.

OH GEE - IT'S IN THE BACK OF THE NET!

(Some Celtic own-goal gaffes)

Jock Stein had long been an admirer of Frank Munro, who had played for Dundee United and Aberdeen before joining Wolves in 1968, so the defender was pretty much a veteran when he arrived on loan in 1977.

With that experience in mind, he was made captain on his debut for the visit of St Mirren but put a black mark on the day by opening the scoring on the hour-mark for the Paisley side.

Tom McAdam equalised but a 20-year-old Billy Stark also scored for the visitors to make it a debut to forget for the new Bhoy.

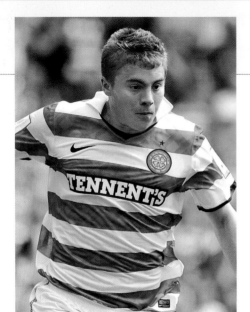

James Forrest

| Wall | **Info** | Photos | + |

About Me 🖊 Edit

Basic Info

Position: Winger	Born: Glasgow
Squad: 49	Height: 5'9"
D.O.B: 07/07/91	Signed: 30/08/09

Career

Debut: v Motherwell (h) 4-0 (SPL) 01/05/10
Previous Clubs: Celtic Youth

Darren O'Dea

| Wall | **Info** | Photos | + |

About Me 🖊 Edit

Basic Info

Position: Defender	Born: Dublin, Ireland
Squad Number: 48	Height: 6'1"
D.O.B: 04/02/87	Signed: 01/08/05

Career

Debut: v St Mirren (h) 2-0 (SLC) 19/09/06
Previous Clubs: Celtic Youth

Andreas Hinkel

| Wall | **Info** | Photos | + |

About Me 🖊 Edit

Basic Info

Position: Right-back	Born: Backnang, Germany
Squad Number: 2	Height: 6'0"
D.O.B: 26/03/82	Signed: 04/01/08

Career

Debut: v Stirling Albion (h) 3-1 (SC) 12/01/08
Previous Clubs: Seville, VfB Stuttgart

Scott Brown

| Wall | Info | Photos | + |

About Me   ✎ Edit

Basic Info

Position: Midfielder   Born: Hill o' Beath, Scotland
Squad Number: 8   Height: 5'10"
D.O.B: 25/06/85   Signed: 01/07/07

Career

Debut: v Kilmarnock (h) 0-0 (SPL) 05/08/07
Previous Clubs: Hibernian

Mark Wilson

| Wall | Info | Photos | + |

About Me   ✎ Edit

Basic Info

Position: Full-back   Born: Glasgow, Scotland
Squad Number: 12   Height: 5'10"
D.O.B: 05/06/84   Signed: 16/01/06

Career

Debut: v Dundee United (h) 3-3 (SPL) 28/01/06
Previous Clubs: Dundee United

Beram Kayal

| Wall | Info | Photos | + |

About Me   ✎ Edit

Basic Info

Position: Midfielder   Born: Jadeidi, Israel
Squad Number:33   Height: 5'10"
D.O.B: 02/05/88   Signed: 29/07/10

Career

Debut: N/A
Previous Clubs: Maccabi Haifa

29

Search 🔍

Paul McGowan

Wall | **Info** | **Photos** | **+**

About Me ✎ Edit

Basic Info

Position: Centre-Forward
Squad Number: 55
D.O.B: 07/10/87

Born: Bellshill, Scotland
Height: 5'7"
Signed: 01/07/05

Career

Debut: v Inverness CT (h) 5-0 (SPL) 15/09/2007
Previous Clubs: Celtic Youths

Paddy McCourt

Wall | **Info** | **Photos** | **+**

About Me ✎ Edit

Basic Info

Position: Winger
Squad Number: 20
D.O.B: 16/12/83

Born: Derry, Ireland
Height: 5'11"
Signed: 19/06/08

Career

Debut: v Hibernian (h) 4-2 (SPL) 25/10/08
Previous Clubs: Rochdale, Shamrock Rovers, Derry City

Shaun Maloney

Wall | **Info** | **Photos** | **+**

About Me ✎ Edit

Basic Info

Position: Striker
Squad Number: 13
D.O.B: 24/01/83

Born: Sarawak, Malaysia
Height: 5'7"
Signed: 22/08/08

Career

Debut: First spell v Rangers (a) 3-0 (SPL) 29/04/01
Second spell v Falkirk (h) 3-0 (SPL) 23/08/08
Previous Clubs: Aston Villa, Celtic, Celtic Youth

Glenn Loovens

Wall   **Info**   Photos   **+**

About Me   ✎ Edit

Basic Info

Position: Centre-back   Born: Doetinchem, Netherlands
Squad Number: 22   Height: 6'2"
D.O.B: 22/10/83   Signed: 16/08/08

Career

Debut: v Falkirk (h) 3-0 (SPL) 23/08/08
Previous Clubs: Cardiff City, De Graafschap (loan),
Excelsior (loan), Feyenoord

Georgios Samaras

Wall   **Info**   Photos   **+**

About Me   ✎ Edit

Basic Info

Position: Centre-forward   Born: Heraklion, Greece
Squad Number: 9   Height: 6'4"
D.O.B: 21/02/85   Signed: 29/01/08

Career

Debut: v Kilmarnock (a) 5-1 (SC) 02/02/08
Previous Clubs: Manchester City, Heerenveen

Marc Crosas

Wall   **Info**   Photos   **+**

About Me   ✎ Edit

Basic Info

Position: Midfielder   Born: Girona, Spain
Squad Number: 17   Height: 5'8"
D.O.B: 09/01/88   Signed: 01/08/09

Career

Debut: v Falkirk (h) 3-0 (SPL) 23/08/08
Previous Clubs: Lyon (loan), Barcelona

Marc-Antoine Fortune

| Wall | **Info** | Photos | **+** |

About Me   🖊 Edit

Basic Info

Position: Striker   Born: Cayenne, French Guiana
Squad Number: 10   Height: 6'0"
D.O.B: 02/07/81   Signed: 09/07/09

Career

Debut: v Dinamo Moscow (h) 0-1 (UCL) 29/07/09
Previous Clubs: West Bromwich Albion (loan),
Nancy, Utrecht, Stade Brest,

Niall McGinn

| Wall | **Info** | Photos | **+** |

About Me   🖊 Edit

Basic Info

Position: Winger   Born: Dungannon, Ireland
Squad: 14   Height: 5'10"
D.O.B: 20/07/87   Signed: 01/01/09

Career

Debut: v Dundee United (h) 1-1 (SPL)12/11/09 (h)
Previous Clubs: Derry City, Dungannon Swifts

Lukasz Zaluska

| Wall | **Info** | Photos | **+** |

About Me   🖊 Edit

Basic Info

Position: Goalkeeper   Born: Wysokie Mazowieckie, Poland
Squad Number: 24   Height: 6'4"
D.O.B: 16/06/82   Signed: 01/06/09

Career

Debut: v Falkirk (a) 4-0 (LC) 23/09/09
Previous Clubs: Dundee United, Korona Kielce,
Legia Warsaw, Stomil Olsztyn, Zryw Zielona Gora,
Sparta Obornoki, MSP Szamotuly, Ruch Wysokie
Mazowieckie

Jos Hooiveld

Wall **Info** **Photos** **+**

About Me   ✎ Edit

Basic Info

Position: Centre-back	Born: Zeijen, Holland
Squad: 6	Height: 6'3"
D.O.B: 22/04/83	Signed: 11/01/10

Career

Debut: v Hamilton (a) 1-0 (SPL) 30/01/10
Previous Clubs: AIK Stockholm, Heerenveen,
Kapfenberg, Inter Turku

Thomas Rogne

Wall **Info** **Photos** **+**

About Me   ✎ Edit

Basic Info

Position: Centre-back	Born: Norway
Squad: 25	Height: 6'3"
D.O.B: 29/06/90	Signed: 20/01/10

Career

Debut: v Hearts (h) 2-0 (SPL) 20/02/10
Previous Clubs: FC Stabaek

Dominic Cervi

Wall **Info** **Photos** **+**

About Me   ✎ Edit

Basic Info

Position: Goalkeeper	Born: Oklahoma, USA
Squad Number: 47	Height: 6'6"
D.O.B: 09/07/86	Signed: 01/07/09

Career

Debut: N/A
Previous Clubs: Michigan Bucks

🎽 ⚽ 🏴 | Search 🔍

Ki Sung-Yueng

Wall | **Info** | Photos | **+**

About Me ✏️ Edit

Basic Info

Position: Midfielder	Born: South Korea
Squad: 18	Height: 6'2"
D.O.B: 24/01/89	Signed: 01/01/10

Career

Debut: v Falkirk (h) 1-1 (SPL) 16/01/10
Previous Clubs: FC Seoul

Josh Thompson

Wall | **Info** | Photos | **+**

About Me ✏️ Edit

Basic Info

Position: Centre-back	Born: Bolton, England
Squad: 38	Height: 6'4"
D.O.B: 25/02/91	Signed: August 2009

Career

Debut: v Falkirk (h) 1-1 (SPL) 16/01/2010
Previous Clubs: Stockport County

Morten Rasmussen

Wall | **Info** | Photos | **+**

About Me ✏️ Edit

Basic Info

Position: Centre-forward	Born: Copenhagen, Denmark
Squad: 19	Height: 6'1"
D.O.B: 31/01/85	Signed: 01/01/10

Career

Debut: v Hibernian (h) 1-2 (SPL) 27/01/10
Previous Clubs: FC Brondby, AGF

Joe Ledley

Wall **Info** **Photos** **+**

About Me   ✎ Edit

Basic Info

Position: Midfielder   Born: Cardiff, Wales
Squad Number: 16   Height: 6'0"
D.O.B: 21/01/87   Signed: 12/07/10

Career

Debut: v SC Braga (a) 0 3, (UCL) 28/07/10
Previous Clubs: Cardiff City

Charlie Mulgrew

Wall **Info** **Photos** **+**

About Me   ✎ Edit

Basic Info

Position: Defender   Born: Glasgow, Scotland
Squad Number: 21   Height: 6'2"
D.O.B: 06/03/86   Signed: 01/07/10

Career

Debut: v SC Braga (a) 0-3, (UCL) 28/07/10
Previous Clubs: Aberdeen, Southend (loan), Wolves,
Dundee United (loan), Celtic

Cha Du-Ri

Wall **Info** **Photos** **+**

About Me   ✎ Edit

Basic Info

Position: Midfielder   Born: Frankfurt am Main, Germany
Squad Number: 11   Height: 5'11"
D.O.B: 25/07/80   Signed: 02/07/10

Career

Debut: v SC Braga (a) 0-3, (UCL) 28/07/10
Previous Clubs: Freiburg, Koblenz, Mainz, Eintracht
Frankfurt, Eintracht Frankfurt (loan), Arminia,
Bielefeld (loan), Bayer Leverkusen

35

Search 🔍

Daryl Murphy

| Wall | **Info** | Photos | ✚ |

About Me   ✏ Edit

Basic Info

Position: Striker   Born: Waterford, Ireland
Squad Number: 27   Height: 6'2"
D.O.B: 15/03/83   Signed: 15/07/10

─────────────── Career ───────────────

Debut: v SC Braga (a) 0-3, (UCL) 28/07/10
Previous Clubs: Ipswich Town (loan), Sheffield
Wednesday (loan), Sunderland, Waterford

Efrain Juarez

| **Wall** | Info | Photos | ✚ |

About Me   ✏ Edit

Basic Info

Position: Defender   Born: Mexico City, Mexico
Squad Number: 4   Height: 5'10"
D.O.B: 22/02/88   Signed: 17/07/10

─────────── Career ───────────

Debut: v SC Braga (a) 0-3, (UCL) 28/07/10
Previous Clubs: Pumas UNAM

Milan Misun

| Wall | **Info** | Photos | ✚ |

About Me   ✏ Edit

Basic Info

Position: Central-defender   Born: Pribram, Czech Republic
Squad Number: 15   Height: 6'2"
D.O.B: 21/02/90   Signed: 01/01/09

─────────────── Career ───────────────

Debut: N/A
Previous Clubs: FK Pribram

Daniel Majstorovic

Wall | **Info** | Photos | ✚

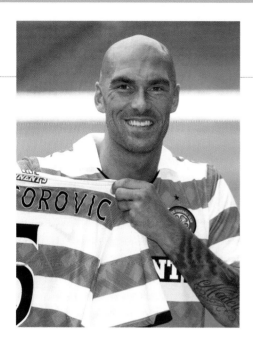

About Me   ✎ Edit

Basic Info

Position: Defender	Born: Malmo, Sweden
Squad Number: 5	Height: 6'4"
D.O.B: 05/04/77	Signed: 16/08/10

Career

Debut: N/A
Previous Clubs: AEK Athens, FC Twente, Malmo FF,
Vasteras, Fortuna Koln, IF Brommapojkarna

Paul Slane

Wall | **Info** | Photos | ✚

About Me   ✎ Edit

Basic Info

Position: Winger	Born: Glasgow
Squad: 30	Height: 5'10"
D.O.B: 25/11/91	Signed 31/01/10

Career

Debut: N/A
Previous Clubs: Motherwell

Gary Hooper

Wall | **Info** | Photos | ✚

About Me   ✎ Edit

Basic Info

Position: Striker	Born: Loughton, England
Squad Number: 88	Height: 5'9"
D.O.B: 26/01/88	Signed: 27/07/10

Career

Debut: N/A
Previous Clubs: Scunthorpe United, Hereford United
(loan), Leyton Orient (loan), Southend United, Grays
Athletic.

Green Cuisine

NO stone is left unturned to ensure that Celtic's players are in optimum condition before a match – and a vital part of that process involves their dietary habits.

By eating correctly, players can train harder, reduce the risk of injury and illness, and perform better over 90 minutes.

Responsible for deciding what goes on the players' plate on a daily basis are Celtic's senior chefs Allan McNaught and Mo Gordon.

Their task is not merely a job of cooking and preparation. At a top-class football club like Celtic, it also involves plenty of careful planning and the application of sports science.

Here Allan and Mo give us an insight into how they keep the Celtic players in tip-top condition on a normal day at Lennoxtown.

We are at Lennoxtown at 7am to take deliveries, prepare the kitchen and start making breakfast for 9.30am. We have got to make sure the players get some proteins and sugars into them first thing before training.

We want to try and find a balance, so ideally we want a third of their plates to be carbohydrates, a third to be energy sugars and a third to be proteins. They will get the options of scrambled eggs, beans, toast, yoghurts, cereals, jams and honey.

Breakfast finishes at 10.30am. They are not allowed to eat 40 minutes before training begins as there is a window of one hour between eating and training for the food to take effect.

We prepare lunch from about 10am onwards and it will go out from around 12.15pm and it will be designed to help them recover after training. We try and include proteins, carbohydrates and sugars again. They get the sugars from fruit and some natural sugars in the food.

Every day we have a new menu. We always try and have the basics of vegetables, potatoes, rice and chicken, which are sources of everything you need. The other things we try and do is have a pasta dish, along with beef, lamb or fish dish so they are always getting a balance of every food. Some of the players have religious beliefs as well so they don't eat certain meats, so we also have to provide another source of food that they can eat.

Injured players, however, can't eat proteins and carbohydrates. They have got to eat red meat because they are good for iron intake, which produces a hormone that helps you recover quicker.

If there are players training in the afternoon, we will leave out cereal bars, nuts and raisins to try and get energy back into them.

The younger players from the Academy who come in at night will get chicken and pasta dishes. That is simply a training food for them, while for the first-team players it's a combination of everything; training, recovery and energy.

A RECIPE FOR SUCCESS

Celtic's senior chefs, Allan McNaught and Mo Gordon, have designed a menu for budding Hoops stars of the future which provides a healthy mix of proteins, carbohydrates and sugars.

MENU

Breakfast

Toast and beans/scrambled egg Or cereal, yoghurt, fruit

Lunch

Chargrilled chicken or pasta with a tomato, pesto or mushroom sauce Fish and rice.

Dinner

Meat, potatoes and plenty of vegetables/vegetarian lasagne or pasta arrabiata.

CELTIC women's team made history in May by winning their first ever piece of silverware.

The Hoops captured the Scottish Women's Premier League Cup with an emphatic 4-1 victory over Spartans at Ainslie Park, Edinburgh, thanks to braces from Christie Murray and Jo Love.

After a massive celebratory huddle in the centre circle involving the entire squad, team captain, Amy McDonald had the honour of lifting the side's first ever trophy.

No-one there could have argued that Robert Docherty's side were not deserved winners of the competition, after a commanding performance on the night and overcoming some of the best teams in the country en-route to the final.

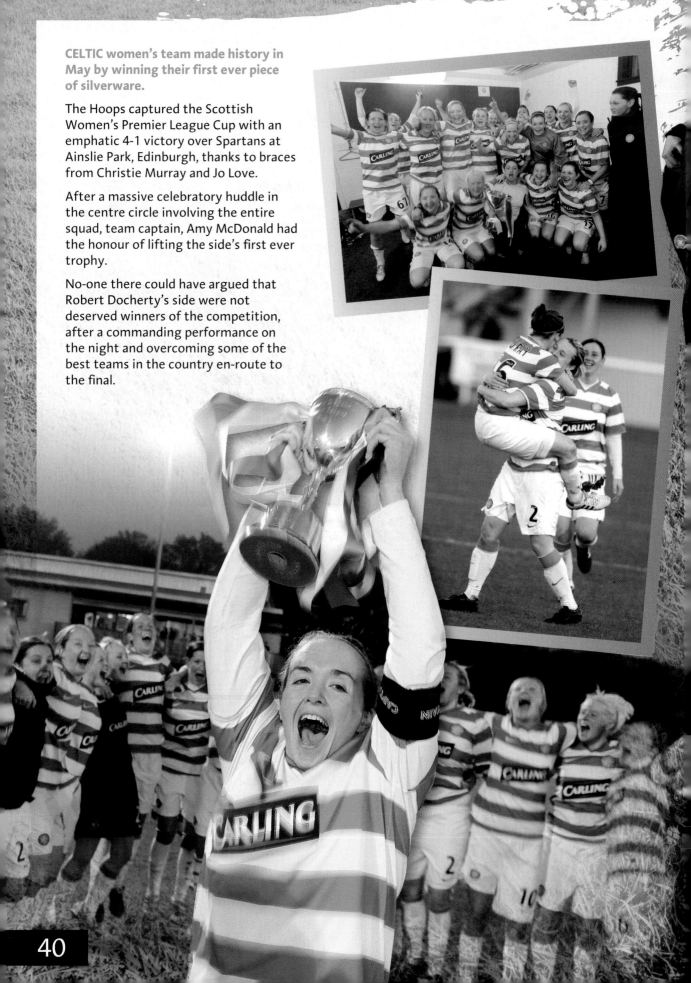

In the opening round of the tournament, Suzanne Grant notched a double and Jo Love also found the net to dispose of top-flight side Boroughmuir 3-1.

The quarter-final draw had paired Celtic with fierce rivals Glasgow City – the cup holders. City took the lead, but Love slotted home to bring the scores level in the closing minutes, forcing extra time. And a 35-yard strike from Grant in the 102nd minute secured a dramatic win.

In the semi-final, Aberdeen were swept aside in a 5-0 thumping with Grant netting a hat-trick. Love and Murray were the other goal-scorers who set-up the final with Spartans.

And, with the Hoops now firmly established as one of the top sides in the country, the League Cup triumph will surely be the first of many for the Ghirls over the coming seasons.

Who is your favourite singer or group? Do you have the same CDs as your Celtic favourites?

It's time to find out in the second part of our entertainment head-to-head with the players.

Marc Crosas

What's your favourite piece of music on your iPod?

Coldplay. I've got all of their CDs in the same folder.

Who is your favourite group/artist of all time?

Coldplay again. I have seen them many times live and I think they are brilliant. They have quiet songs and other ones with more action and rhythm.

What was the best gig you have ever been to?

Apart from Coldplay, the Killers in Barcelona were amazing. I saw them in the place where they play basketball in Barcelona.

What is your favourite film?

The Motorcycle Diaries. I think it was out around four years ago. I liked the story of Che Guevara and what he did, not just for his country and Cuba, for the whole of South America. And I think the actor, Gael Garcia Bernal is amazing. And, after I watched that movie, I thought one day I would like do the same trip they did on the motorcycle.

What TV programme do you never miss?

Obviously, I could say Spanish TV programmes. But, over here, the British programme I never miss is *Friday Night with Jonathan Ross* because I think he is funny.

Scott Brown

What's your favourite piece of music on your iPod?

Up-to-date music, whatever is in the charts at the time.

Who is your favourite group/artist of all time?

The Killers or 50 Cent.

What was the best gig you have ever been to?

I've never been to a gig.

What is your favourite film?

Avatar.

What TV programme do you never miss?

Prison Break and *Friends,* I still watch them now.

Paul Slane

What's your favourite piece of music on your iPod?

Probably some good rave tunes. Anything with a right good dance beat. I just like that type of music.

Who is your favourite group/ artist of all time?

I would probably say Oasis. I think they are brilliant. It's just unfortunate they have split up now.

What was the best gig you have ever been to?

I have only been to one and it was Robbie Williams. I used to love him and went to see him with my sister. That was brilliant. I think I was about 14, so it's quite embarrassing really.

What is your favourite film?

I love *Rocky*. It's brilliant. The first one is just so inspirational.

What TV programme do you never miss?

The only thing I would say is *Lost*. I just got into the box set and got quite addicted to it and kept watching it. So that would be the only thing.

When the playing pool broke up for the summer, your Celtic Annual grabbed the opportunity to sneak into the club's Lennoxtown training base to find out what it's like when it's a bit quieter.

This is what we found...

WEIGHT IN LINE... Where to work out with the best view around.

GYM'LL FIX IT... This is where the Hoops get really fit.

BOARDROOM DRILL... Ross Robertson with some final touches before the start of a new season.

ROOM WITH A VIEW... Mark Henderson of the Celtic media team with another scoop.

POOL SECRETARIES... Allison More and Christine Brooks making sure everything goes to plan.

PRESS HERE... The man from the View in the hot seat before the latest media conference.

GRAND ENTRANCE... Where you are hail, hailed on arrival at Lennoxtown.

MULTICOLOURED BOOTROOM... Film and TV aren't the only things that have moved from black and white to Technicolour down through the years.

CLEAN SWEEP... Karen Leneghan and Edwina Tominey make sure everything is in pristine condition.

WEDDED BLISS... The only married couple at Lennoxtown, Jim and Edwina Tominey.

Colour me in!

Shaun Maloney is wearing the Hoops here and we want you to work your magic and bring this pic to life with your crayons, ink markers or paints – by the way, Shaun's wearing his RED boots in this game.

Guess Who?

1

2

3

6

5

4

Answers on pages 62/63

OH GEE - IT'S IN THE BACK OF THE NET!

(Some Celtic own-goal gaffes)

It's par for the course that a defender will score an own goal at some point but spare a thought for Celt Andy Lynch who scored two own goals in two minutes, the 85th and the 87th, when Celtic lost 3-0 to Motherwell at Fir Park in April 1977.

Still, the Hoops lifted the title three days later at Easter Road and then Andy Lynch scored the winner in the Scottish Cup final on May 7.

The Celts then paraded the trophy in their last game of the season on May 10 – at Fir Park.

Football Firsts

IT'S time to catch up with some more of your Celtic heroes and find out how they started on the road to Paradise.

Shaun Maloney

What was the first football match you attended?

It was Aberdeen v Celtic at Pittodrie. I just remember we missed two penalties during the game and lost 3-2. We were wearing the new black away strip for the first time.

What was the first football strip you ever wore?

I think it would probably be an Arsenal away strip as my dad was a big Arsenal fan. It was a criss-cross pattern with JVC on the front.

Do you remember the first pair of football boots you had?

The first pair would be Diadora Baggios. I would have been about seven or eight.

Who was the first player you really admired?

It would probably be Henrik when I was younger as he was the focal point of the team that I supported. He scored in the majority of the games that he played.

What was the first team you ever played for?

St Joseph's Primary in Aberdeen. I would have been in primary four or five.

Niall McGinn

What was the first football match you attended?

The first game was Celtic v Rangers. I think I was only 14 and Alan Thompson scored the winner in the 89th minute. It was a brilliant game.

What was the first football strip you ever wore?

I had a few Gaelic tops, but my first football jersey was a Celtic shirt. It was the home strip and it was around 1996 or 1997 when I got it.

Do you remember the first pair of football boots you had?

My first boots were a pair of Mizunos. I was probably only around five or six when I got them.

Who was the first player you really admired?

Probably Eric Cantona. I just loved watching him. He was a character on and off the pitch and just a great player.

What was the first team you ever played for?

That was Dungannon United youth back home. I started with them when I was about eight or nine. I just started going to the fun weeks and then pushed into the U10s and 11s all the way up to the first team.

Scott Brown

What was the first football match you attended?

I was a ball boy at Cowdenbeath when I was about seven. My mate was a ball boy and a space was going so I went for it. The first game was East Stirling or Stirling Albion, I can't remember. As a fan, the first game I went to was Queen's Park v Cowdenbeath. I was about 11 or 12 and we got the bus through to Hampden, it was a great day. I think that was the only bus that went though!

What was the first football strip you ever wore?

It was the tartan Scotland strip. It was horrific. Somebody bought me it for Christmas and I was almost embarrassed to wear it because it was so bad, but that was years ago.

Do you remember the first pair of football boots you had?

I had a pair of Puma Kings, the old fashioned, retro boots. It must have been about 1992.

Who was the first player you really admired?

Maradona

What was the first team you ever played for?

Beath Centre, but they don't exist anymore.

Paul McGowan

What was the first football match you attended?

I think it was Celtic v Hearts at Celtic Park. It was around the time that Di Canio and Cadete were playing.

What was the first football strip you ever wore?

My first strip was the Celtic Bumble Bee top. My mum got me it.

Do you remember the first pair of football boots you had?

The first set of football boots I remember getting was a pair of Adidas Predator. I would have been around 10 when I got them.

Who was the first player you really admired?

Henrik Larsson. He was a brilliant player, great to watch and he was one of the best players to ever play for Celtic.

What was the first team you ever played for?

My first team was Airdrie Boys' Club. I joined them at seven or eight. I stayed with them for two years before I went to Celtic Boys' Club.

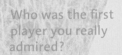

CELTIC Under-19s swept all before them last season, lifting both the league championship and the SFA Youth Cup during a memorable week in April.

A remarkable run of seven successive victories had already put Tommy McIntyre and Stevie Frail's side out of sight at the top of the table by the time they faced Aberdeen at a sun-kissed Lennoxtown.

But they held off any celebrations until making it eight wins on the trot, with Callum McGregor grabbing the only goal of the game in a 1-0 triumph.

The final whistle was the signal for joyous scenes as players and coaching staff poured on to the pitch and embraced one another.

Then, on the following Wednesday night, the young Hoops produced a tremendous display to beat Rangers 2-0 at Hampden in the cup final and collect their second piece of silverware.

Sean Fitzharris opened the scoring in the second-half with a wonderful strike from 20 yards, before Filip Twardzik sealed the win with a diving header.

In front of around 7,500 supporters, skipper Matty Hughes lifted the cup to cap off a magnificent season for the side.

It had been four years since the youths had captured either trophy and they were given the honour of celebrating their success in front of the Celtic support.

During the final home fixture of the season against Motherwell, they were presented with the league championship trophy at half-time, before taking the richly-deserved acclaim of the crowd as they paraded both cups around the stadium.

One player who wasn't able to take part in those celebrations was James Forrest. The talented winger had been a key figure for the U19s and had been promoted to the bench by Neil Lennon.

But he rounded off a perfect week for the youth set-up by scoring a brilliant goal on his first-team debut just six minutes after entering the fray.

Celtic –
The Community Club

SINCE its launch in June 2003, Celtic in the Community has coached over 2.5million children, teenagers and adults from Scotland, Ireland and beyond.

And now, nearly 7,000 young people participate in Celtic in the Community programmes each week.

There are many and varied courses for both boys and girls from four-years-old upwards including train-only courses, residential and non-residential courses, and the matchday experience when you can also take in a Celtic home game.

And, of course, as you can see here, there is always the chance that you might meet one or two of your Celtic heroes to give you a wee coaching tip or two.

Celtic's community courses have been a tremendous success, with more than

30 players coming from the Community Academy programmes in to the club's Development Centres and full Academy in recent years.

The Play for Celtic programme has teams that train each week and then wear the famous Hoops at the weekend, representing Celtic in leagues throughout Scotland.

The Girls Youth Academy also have a large grassroots programme and talented players are progressed into the Girls Academy with around 40 coming through so far.

52

Shaun Maloney said of last year's summer coaching courses:

" I know the summer coaching courses have already been a great success and they always provide a fun football environment for kids of all ages.

It is the dream of many kids to play for Celtic and these courses have also shown that they allow young players to develop towards the club's full Academy and perhaps even further success with Celtic.

I hope everyone taking part in these courses has a great time. "

For further information see www.celticfc.net
email: communitycoaching@celticfc.co.uk
or tel: 0871 226 1888* (option 5).

* Calls cost up to 10p per minute, telecoms provider dependent. Mobile and other provider charges may vary.

Dot-to-Dot

Join up all of the dots in this picture and see if you can identify the Celt.
The solution is on page 63.

THE CELTIC FOOTBALL CLUB
1888

✱ Start Point

54

Quiz

WHAT'S THE CONNECTION?

Here's a list of some Celtic names from down through the decades but what do they have in common apart from signing for Celtic?

Barney Battles	Shaun Maloney	Willie Groves	Barney Crossan
Frank McAvennie	Charlie Nicholas	Tom Dunbar	Johnny Campbell
Bertie Auld	Tommy McInally	Peter Dowds	John Divers
Andy Walker	Vic Davidson	Bobby Lennox	Willie Fernie

The answer is on pages 63.

OH GEE - IT'S IN THE BACK OF THE NET!
(Some Celtic own-goal gaffes)

Henrik Larsson scored some pretty amazing goals at Celtic Park and you could talk all day about the more memorable ones.

There was his strike on the day the 10 was stopped, his wonderfully sublime chip in the 6-2 game or what about his last ever goal for the Hoops at Celtic Park?

Then again, what about his first ever goal at Paradise – well, believe it or not, that was an own goal.

Austrian side Tirol Innsbruck were the opponents in the UEFA Cup and, despite Henrik's input, the Celts won 6-3 on the night and 7-5 on aggregate.

Huddle Online

Since its launch in January, 2010, the Huddle Online has allowed Celtic supporters worldwide to catch-up on all the latest news and action at the club.

Broadcast on Channel 67, the club's audio and video channel, the daily magazine show is packed with exclusive interviews with players past and present, breaking news, highlights and analysis, and classic footage.

Here, Gregor Kyle, presenter of the Huddle Online, gives an idea to how the programme is put together on a normal working week. As we discover, it's a real team effort.

THE (H)UDDLE ONLINE

MONDAY

Monday is the post-match show, so the first thing we do is head to Lennoxtown and interview a player who was involved in the weekend's game. Then we come back to the studio and film the post-match analysis piece, usually with Tony Hamilton. At the same time, the multi-media team will put together the highlights package, the post-match press conference and game analysis and it's all edited. Then, there is the stuff you have to do everyday. This involves filming links, the web team building up the daily Huddle Online page and uploading the programme on to the site. We try to have it all done for 4pm.

TUESDAY

It's a similar process to Monday. You are still looking back at the weekend, but are now looking forward as well. We will usually head up to Lennoxtown and interview a player, before coming back to put the show together. Often, we will also cover the U19s, looking at their game from the weekend. Any day of the week, we also have to keep on top of any news within the club, which could be anything ranging from club charity and community events — so those need to be filmed and covered too.

WEDNESDAY

This is the Celtic View day, so that means there is a 10-minute piece in the studio with me speaking to editor Paul Cuddihy or one of the reporters. We will cover the week's news with the View and what else is happening in the Celtic world. During the week we will also put together some of our exclusive features such as Faithful Through and Through, in which former players look back at their experiences, or the Where are They Now feature. Something we do regularly as well is interviewing former Celts who may have stopped by at the stadium.

THURSDAY

This is the manager's show. So we would head up to Lennoxtown for 8.30 am to chat to him first thing in the morning, covering the previous week's game, the forthcoming match at the weekend and any breaking news during the week. These are longer interviews, usually lasting 15 minutes. During the days we are up at Lennoxtown we are also carrying out interviews with the youth and reserve players. After that, we are back up the studio to edit and film the show. Each day of the week, I will also need to check e-mails from fans getting in touch with the programme. Regularly, we run competitions for supporters such as Goal of the Month.

FRIDAY

This is the pre-match show, so we will interview a player – usually at Lennoxtown – and film the media conference with the manager and player. We will also show a previous meeting with the team we are up against. If there are any special events on at the weekend, such as birthdays or landmarks, we will also show some classic footage from the club archives which date back to 1922. It will also be the time we start planning ahead for the following week.

To see the Huddle Online, check out www.celticfc.net

NOW it's time for part two of our insight into what the Celts from far-flung corners of the globe miss about their homeland.

Milan Misun

What village/town/city are you from?

I am from a small village called Pribram with about 35,000 people, which is about 60km from Prague.

What do you miss most about it?

I miss all my family, my friends and my girlfriend.

Are you recognised when you go back there?

Some people from the Czech Republic send me a postcard and I send them a photo but that is all – but they're not from my village.

What did you think about Scotland before you came here and what do you think now?

I didn't really know much about Scotland before I came here. I knew that Celtic and Rangers were big clubs. But it's a nice country. I like it here.

Who is your local team and did you support them?

I played for FK Pribram in back home and supported them.

Morten Rasmussen

What village/town/city are you from?

A little village outside of Aarhus, which is the second biggest city in Denmark. So it's about five or six miles from the city centre.

What do you miss most about it?

When you are playing in another country you miss your family and friends, but that's okay as you get some new friends where you play.

Are you recognised when you go back there?

Yeah, but I have played in Brondby before I came here which is the biggest club in Denmark, so it's not like here but it was close to it.

What did you think about Scotland before you came here and what do you think now?

I knew Scotland was part of the UK, and knew the mentality was like that of the Danish so that was a good thing for me to come to a place where the mentality was the same. I knew Celtic were a big club. Now I still have the same opinion.

Who is your local team and did you support them?

My local team was Aarhus. When I was young I played in the village that I came from and then I changed to Aarhus where I played as a professional player, so yeah I still support them.

Georgios Samaras

What village/town/city are you from?

Heraklion, the capital city of Crete.

What do you miss most about it?

The sun. It's totally different from here. Here it's cloudy and rainy and when you have a nice day, you see the sun and then 10 minutes later it's raining. I do like the wind and rain but some days I need the sun as well. And in Crete you have the sun around 300 days a year.

Are you recognised when you go back there?

Yes. You live in a city where everyone knows you. Here, I try to stay home and away from the lifestyle around football and just try and focus on my game. But when you go home, you cannot stay in. You have to go out and it's something you get used to. People will come and talk to you or maybe look at you. But there is nothing you can do but just enjoy it and try to give some happiness to people if they want your autograph. It's a part of football you must accept.

What did you think about Scotland before you came here and what do you think now?

Everyone was telling me about Scotland, how it was a beautiful country with really nice places, with hills, castles and things. Sometimes it would be difficult to imagine in your mind. You also have films like *Braveheart* and you try to learn some of the history. Everyone was also telling me that Edinburgh was one of the beautiful cities in Europe. So I had an idea of Scotland before I came. And I totally agree with what people said. Scotland is a beautiful country. There are so many places you can go, relax and enjoy the countryside. Glasgow is a nice city, but I think Edinburgh is something magic.

Who is your local team and did you support them?

The local team is OFI. They were the team I started playing with when I was 10. I was there until I was 16 when I moved to Holland. They are the team I still support and love.

Thomas Rogne

What village/town/city are you from?

A suburb of Oslo called Baerum. It's quite a big place, there are probably around 120,000 people who live there.

What do you miss most about it?

I miss friends, my girlfriend and family the most. It's also where I lived my whole life so you are always going miss something about that.

Are you recognised when you go back there?

No, well maybe a few people. But it's not as intense and not as big a deal back in Norway as it is here.

What did you think about Scotland before you came here and what do you think now?

To be honest I didn't know too much before I came. So I didn't have many expectations. But I like it. I heard some people saying the weather is bad, but I actually think it's quite good. So I enjoy Scotland very much.

Who is your local team and did you support them?

It was Stabaek, so, yeah, I supported them my whole life.

CELTIC Charity Fund has launched fundraising schemes to co-ordinate, support and celebrate the wonderful charitable efforts of Celtic supporters and employees alike.

Celtic staff and fans across the globe make huge efforts to help those less fortunate and these new schemes allow us to make an even bigger impact as a collective unit - the Celtic Family.

Basically, any Celtic employee, Celtic Supporters' Club or individual fan undertaking such activities to raise monies for a registered charity close to their hearts can now direct them through Celtic Charity Fund. The total will be topped up by 25 per cent (before any Gift Aid Calculations) and the cumulative amount will be donated, on behalf of the supporter or member of staff, to the nominated charity. It's that simple.

The only stipulation is that the selected charity falls within at least one of Celtic Charity Fund's key themes:-

Principal

- Charities in support of children's needs
- Community action on drugs
- Projects that develop and promote religious and ethnic harmony

Subsidiary

- Supporting the homeless
- Helping the unemployed
- Support and research for projects aiding the afflictions of illness, famine and innocent families within areas of war

For further information on the schemes, contact Jane Maguire at Celtic Charity Fund on 0141 551 4262 or janemaguire@celticfc.co.uk

Runners Up

Winning Team

THE Celtic Charity Fund also runs a series of fundraising events on an annual basis, including a five-a-side tournament in which supporters take part.

The Celtic Charity Cup has been running since 2007 and everyone who takes part is a winner as each and every one of them is raising much-needed money for a worthy cause.

Of course, there can only be one winner of the actual trophy and last season's top side was Emerald Isle who came out top of 14 teams from the Champions League-style groups.

Celtic youth coach Stevie Frail was on hand to present the trophy after Emerald Isle beat The A Team 3-1 in the final.

ANOTHER magnificent Celtic Charity Fund project last season saw 200 Celtic supporters commit to the ultimate leap of faith...

They jumped off the roof of the Main Stand at Celtic Park all in the aid of charity with the main beneficiary being the Cystic Fibrosis Trust, while the remaining half of the money raised was divided between other Celtic charities.

Among those who took the plunge in the charity abseil was the *Celtic View's* Laura Brannan who went to the extreme in getting a new angle on the stadium for the magazine's report on the high-flying fundraisers.

Answers

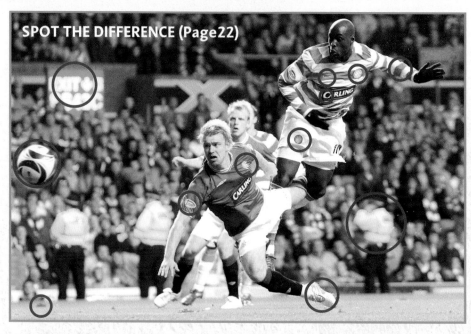

SPOT THE DIFFERENCE (Page22)

CELTIC QUIZ

ANSWERS (Page 23)

01 Tottenham Hotspur 0-2 Celtic in the Wembley Cup.

02 He kept a clean sheet in a 4-0 CIS Cup win over Falkirk.

03 Aiden McGeady scored twice in the 3-1 win over Aberdeen.

04 It was a 5-2 SPL win over St Johnstone in the first home league match of the term.

05 The games were against Motherwell and SV Hamburg.

06 James Forrest, Marc-Antoine Fortune, Diomanse Kamara, Robbie Keane, Paddy McCourt, Niall McGinn, Paul McGowan, Morten Rasmussen, Josh Thompson and Zheng Zhi.

07 He hit a treble in a 3-0 Scottish Cup win over Kilmarnock.

08 The Hoops used a total of 32 players in all competitions.

09 Spurs, Arsenal and Al-Ahly.

10 They played in a total of five capitals - Edinburgh, Cardiff, Moscow, Vienna and London.

WORDSEARCH ANSWERS (Page 27)

01 RobbieKeane

02 SouthAfrica

03 Eleven

04 BumbleBee

05 UnitedStates

06 ZhengZhi

07 Penalty

08 Three

09 Whistle

A	D	E	N	A	E	K	E	I	B	B	O	R
G	J	L	Q	E	T	U	O	P	Z	C	S	B
M	Z	W	R	Y	I	P	E	S	F	E	O	H
E	H	X	V	N	Q	N	E	T	T	E	U	U
L	E	O	A	D	A	D	G	A	J	B	T	L
T	N	Q	R	L	U	P	T	S	G	E	H	K
S	G	E	T	X	B	S	Q	E	Y	L	A	O
I	Z	Y	V	S	D	G	K	Z	V	B	F	M
H	H	N	C	E	S	E	F	Y	J	M	R	N
W	I	P	T	O	L	K	N	H	Y	U	I	G
S	R	I	F	Y	H	E	K	Q	P	B	C	X
X	N	U	H	A	L	Z	J	I	T	V	A	R
U	C	Z	A	X	U	T	H	T	H	R	E	E